Cormorant Time

A Madman's Journal
Poems Written in a Time of Fever

BY JOHN WULP

FIRST EDITION
ISBN 978-0-692-80513-8

PUBLISHED BY PHILIP CONKLING & ASSOCIATES
CAMDEN, MAINE

All photographs and paintings by John Wulp with the exception of the Marine Barracks group photo on page 27, courtesy of RIDEOUT PHOTOS, WASHINGTON, DC, 1952

When, spite of cormorant devouring Time,
The endeavor of this present breath may buy
That honour which shall bate his scythe's keen edge
And make us heirs of all eternity.

WILLIAM SHAKESPEARE
Love's Labours Lost
ACT 1, SCENE 1

APPLE BLOSSOM, 1998

Preface

I have known John Wulp for almost two decades. John left the theatre world after years of designing and directing shows on- and off-Broadway. I met him during his tenure as a drama teacher at the North Haven Community School, where he drew out of countless island students a range and depth of talent they otherwise would not have known they had.

In the years since, as neighbors on Vinalhaven, we have shared ferry rides and exchanged snatches of conversations "down street" on such topics as the state of the world, his art, my sons and his faithful dog, Jude. We have had tea together under his apple tree at Stone Farm or in his studio, usually crowded with new works of art on canvas.

Because we are neighbors on a small island, I understood that John's health became increasingly compromised as he entered his 88th year. When John recently pressed into my hands a sheaf of poems he had just started writing, I had no idea what to expect.

From the very first poem I read, and then through the nearly breathless pace he maintained with the next hundred poems he shared, I was shocked by the power of his voice and his relentless search for expression.

John is protean—as all his many admirers and neighbors already know. But his ability to continuously reinvent himself as an artist—even as I write—is both astonishing and inspiring. It's been like watching a fire burn, at turns beautiful, thrilling and uncontrollable.

PHILIP CONKLING
ROCKAWAY, LANES ISLAND

BOOK ONE

Dedicated to James Russek

Cormorant Time

Cormorant time
Is devouring me
Alive
Each day it eats
A part of me
The very heart and soul of me
And yet I feel
More alive
Than I've ever felt before

APRIL 19, 2016

If You Put a Man

If you put a man
Into a house
That had one room
On an island
In Maine
He couldn't go out
He couldn't drive to town
He'd probably go mad
Or write poetry
Maybe both

APRIL 22, 2016

88

Why do poets always have meadows
A copse of wood nearby
A pond, a terrace
A place for afternoon tea
And deep thoughts

I have an old, ruined orchard
And sometimes in spring and summer
I have tea there
Underneath the branches
My trees are more
Than a hundred years old
They're gnarled and twisted
Like crones in a fairy tale
Or a Walt Disney movie

Like my apple trees
I am old and twisted too
The only difference is
Each year, in spring
They put on their best finery
Clothes they wore when they were young
And gambol like children on the lawn
They may seem foolish
In their white frocks
But they know things
About living and dying
And coming to life again
That I shall never know

I've just started school
And already the bell has rung

MARCH 24, 2016

For Jen D.

Hours of disease and death
Small cuts, abrasions
Deep cuts, sea wounds
Infusions, enemas, draining blood
Small talk
Laughter
Occasionally a pitiful sob
Babies, mewling and crying
Cancer
Heart Disease
Dementia
Sexual abuse
Drug addiction
These are the fields through which she walks.
Listening
Patient
Kind
She regards each mortal imperfection as if it were a flower
She teaches us what it means to be human

AUGUST 18, 2016

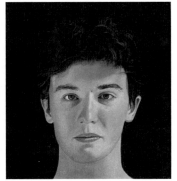

MARCO, I, II, III, 2015

Marco

marcosmainelobster
Is his email address
He cares for lobster
And Maine more than
He cares for me

This past summer
Marco in a blue shirt
Was revelation
Which he did not see
Nor care to be

We pass like strangers
In the night of day
And yet he is the sight
By which I see
He is the vision
Of what I care to be

MARCH 28, 2016

Muse

What good is a muse anyhow
Like the weather
She's unpredictable
She comes and goes
In fits and starts
One never knows
When she might arrive
Or when she will depart

She's moody
The least little thing
Can set her off
It's like walking on eggshells
All the time when she's around
She always wears sneakers
So that she can quietly
Sidle up to you
And, giggling, whisper in your ear
At a garden party
With other people standing round
Embarrassing! I'd say

Her dress is eccentric
You can't show her off to friends
It's like Werner Heisenberg
Appearing in an old fashioned
One piece black bathing suit
At Orienta Beach Club
In the thirties
I can think of a great many people
I would rather know

And yet, poets seem
To have a need for her
However irascible
Think how many fewer books
Some well-written
Some the opposite
We'd have, if not for her

It's a sad commentary
On the poet's need
To have a muse
Bad manners often make
Good poetry

MARCH 28, 2016

Poetry

As the song says
I don't know much
About poetry
Oh, I know a little bit
I know about sonnet form
And dactyls, trochees, spondees and all that
I know about iambic pentameter
And how it corresponds to breath
And how when breath stops
It can easily turn to death
But that's about the extent
Of my knowledge
Although, come to think of it,
It's a fairly large extent

I think, however, there is a song
That wants to be sung
Sometimes you can hear it
In the tree tops
Sometimes in the wind or rain
Sometimes you can hear it
In the ocean
When waves break against a rock
Or lap upon the shore
It is a small voice
Crying like Sycorax in a tree
Beseeching to be let out
Wanting to be caught
In words on paper
The only cage which sets its captives free

I hope that I might be
A recorder of that voice
My own has been stilled so long
It might be a clean receptacle
For unfamiliar sounds
It's not my voice that sings
It is the voice of a stranger
Who sings through me
Strange music
With no notation system
To set it down

Just words
Just simple words
Words as simple
As a word can be
Worlds as complex
As the world can be
What does the world tell us
We are alone
What do words tell us
We are not alone

MARCH 29, 2016

Nobody Calls

Nobody calls
To congratulate you
When you become an artist
There are no telegrams
There's no official announcement
No brass bands play
The silence of the telephone is deafening
If anything you're more alone
Than you were before
If you're lucky
J.R. might take your call

But you know it in your bones
If you're a poet
As Gertrude Stein says
The words come out
At your fingertips
If you're a painter
The painting paints itself
The real skill
Is letting it happen

It's all so simple
Why does it take a lifetime
To learn these things

MARCH 29, 2016

My Neighbor

I have a neighbor
Who's both good and bad
I guess the good outweighs the bad
He's often funny
That's the good part
He's just as often self-involved
That's the bad
He would be the very first to accuse me of the same fault

Mr. Goodhue knows a lot of things
You meet a man
In the parking lot
Who's from Quebec
And is an expert on Arctic Literature
You invite him to tea
For which he does not show up
It turns out Mr. Goodhue knows all
About Arctic Literature
It's maddening but probably true.

He's an expert on birds
But what about me
Aren't I an endangered species too
Whenever I write a poem or play
He says it's silly
Whenever I paint a painting
He tells me not to use white
He says over and over again
That it's a color
Which does not exist in nature
Where would I be without white

Mr. Goodhue has many good qualities
There's no denying that
He shovels my walk when it snows
He unfreezes pipes
But he's usually too busy to chat
He hasn't got time for that
He hardly ever visits
And when he does it's just to say
He has no time to visit
Although he sometimes brings fresh eggs

If you need evidence of the world's indifference
Mr. Goodhue would be
The perfect neighbor
But I have lived near him
For thirty years
And during that time
The world's own indifference
Has been quite sufficient for me
It does not need his help
Thank you

But thank you truly
I do mean that
I could have had
A worse person living next door
One who wouldn't build
His own houses and barns
One who wouldn't plant irises
Or kayak to Brimstone
With dolphins leaping beside

Perhaps it's just impossible
To be a perfect neighbor
Nobody's perfect after all.

A Day Job

Mr. Goodhue speaks
In iambic pentameter and rhyme
Tomorrow's April Fools
All my crocuses
Are lined up in a row
You're speaking poetry, I said
Maybe so, he answered me
I'm not going to give up my day job though
For poetry

MARCH 31, 2016

No Charts

I set out to sea
Without any navigation tools
No charts or compasses
No quadrant to shoot the sun

No matter that we have no guides
The journey's everything
Think what sights we'll see
What squalls and tempests
What enchanted isles

Think of Ulysses
Tied blindfolded to the mast
He knew that he was heading home
He knew his way by heart

We are all voyagers in the dark
Blind from birth and yet we see
The thing is to accept what comes
The thing is to make the most of least

I know I'm headed for disaster
It's inevitable
It's certain as day goes down to night
It's certain as life dwindles into death

APRIL 25, 2016

My Parents

My father loved another young woman
Before he married my mother
His first love died
In the flu epidemic of 1918

After his marriage my father kept
A photograph
Of his former fiancée
On his dresser

Eventually
My mother couldn't stand it any longer
She hid the photograph
My father never said a word

O God, how I hate that woman
My father said to me
When my mother left the room
Sometime before he died

I protested
You mustn't say such things, I said
You're only saying them because you're not feeling well
No, I hate her
Was his firm response.
She's never done anything for anybody
Unless there was something in it for herself
He looked me straight in the eye and added
You know that better than anyone else

MY PARENTS, 1959

How could I respond
What a heavy weight
To lay upon a son
The bitter words of a dying man

Love sometimes succeeds
It more often fails
This was knowledge
I did not need to learn
I knew it at my birth

I never married
I lived alone
Was it gain
Or loss

APRIL 21, 2016

Alan T.

Alan T. wanted to be an actor
He wanted that more than anything
In college he was quite good
As Tom in *The Glass Menagerie*
He also played Edmund in *King Lear*
But I don't recall much about that production
Except for the dreadful costumes
Baggy woolen tights and bulky cloaks
That looked as if they could stand up by themselves
I can remember the director sewing them
In the costume shop
He kept maniacally pushing
Yards and yards of fabric
Through the sewing machine

We drove to Cambridge
In my green convertible
For the Dartmouth-Harvard Football game
The top was down
Even though it was mid-November
John M. and Alan T.
Kept drinking all the way
To keep warm
By the time we reached Cambridge
They were both drunk
They love me in Boston, said Alan T.
As he spilled from the open car

On Friday night before the game
We went to see *The Seagull* in Brattle Hall
A place where I had worked the summer before
Cleaning paint buckets in the scenery shop
In the basement
For twenty-five dollars a week

Luise Rainer played Nina
She was much too old for the part
Her voice was so small
You could hardly hear her
She seemed to hide
Behind the scenery
It was the first Chekhov
I had ever seen
When Nina said
Art is the cross we bear
The words became
A presage
Of my whole life
I've never forgotten them

Alan T. came to visit me
During Christmas vacation
We went to the theatre in New York
Every matinee and evening performance
For a whole week
I can't remember one play we saw

After college Alan T.
Enlisted in the Air Force
He was in the Korean War
One day the men in the observation tower on his base
Were surprised to see
The plane he piloted
Make three perfect orbits
As it flew lower and lower
And eventually sunk into the sea
There were no signs of trouble
No radio messages were received
Alan T. was drowned

I often wonder now
In spite of his great popularity in Boston
Whether Alan T. could have made it as an actor
We'll never know

MAY 2, 2016

Two John M.'s

John M. was a good friend
In college
Perhaps the best
He asked me to room with him
He was so good-looking
I was afraid
As I have so often been
Throughout my life
I refused

After college he enlisted in the Navy
When his tour of duty was finished
He moved to Maine
He became a lobster man
One winter I visited him
In Portland, where he lived
By then he had a wife and two children

On a cold and drizzly December day
I went out with him to haul
I plugged the claws of the lobsters
With yellow wooden pegs
My hands were freezing
I thought my fingers would fall off
After we returned to harbor
And were unloading that day's catch
I took a photograph of him
Wearing black boots and southwester gear
He looked incredibly handsome

LOBSTERING, MAINE, 1955

Going out with John M. to haul
Was my first experience
Of what a lobsterman's life is like
It isn't easy
It's back-breaking work
Back then it didn't pay as much
As it does now

Eventually John M. gave it up
He went to work for IBM
I lost track of him
The next thing I knew
He had divorced his wife
He retired to Spain
Where he lived with another woman

They came to visit me once
By then I myself was living in Maine
It was a homecoming of sorts
John M. had lost all his hair
I kept staring at him trying to see
The handsome young man I'd known
Such a long time ago

Each year he sent me a Christmas card
It was the only contact I had
With my college days
A year ago no postcard came
I feared the worst
I wrote to his Spanish lady friend
To ask what happened
 After several months she wrote back to say
John M. was dead

We barely knew each other at all
Just college and a few brief encounters after that
I can't explain my sense of loss
There is a great emptiness of heart
Where John M. used to be

Now there is a new John M. who types for me
He's good looking too
Although he tries to hide it
Behind a beard and shaggy locks
Do you believe in reincarnation
He fills a hole in my life
Although I know him
No better than I knew
The first John M.

MAY 2, 2016

KP

When I was in Marine boot camp
Parris Island, South Carolina
One of my last chores was KP duty
The cooks put a big steel bowl of fruit punch
Out on the lawn
We fell upon our knees
And lapped it up like dogs
A hazy November day
Scrubby brown grass
A barracks nearby
I've never forgotten that experience
Never in my life
Have I felt more like an animal
Never in my life
Have I felt more content

JUNE 23, 2016

Honor Man

I was honor man
In my platoon
At boot camp
United States Marine Corps
Parris Island
South Carolina

On graduation day
I had to lead the troops
Something I had never done before
We proudly marched
To the parade ground
Where the graduation ceremony
Was to be held
The parade ground
Was on the right
A brick building
Was on the left

Column left
The Second Lieutenant shouted
I knew he had made a mistake
I turned column right
The platoon followed after me
Very good, the Second Lieutenant said
Of course I meant column right

After the ceremony
We marched back to our barracks
Another building loomed in front of us
We could go either way
Column right the Second Lieutenant shouted once again

I knew the barracks
Were on the left
I thought the Second Lieutenant had made a second mistake
I turned column left
This time the platoon
Did not follow me
I was marching on my own

God damn it! the Second Lieutenant yelled
Just because I give a command wrong sometimes
That doesn't mean I always do

It is only now
In writing down these words
I see the fault was not entirely my own
The Second Lieutenant shared it too

Is there any solace in words
I doubt it
Did the Second Lieutenant ever think
Of that hot, shameful day
So branded on my memory
I doubt it

What honor, after all
To have lived so long
Alone
With only myself
To blame

APRIL 19, 2016

The Sunset Parade

I was assigned to duty
At Marine Barracks
Eighth and I Streets
Washington, D.C.

It was the commandant's post
We were the elite troops
Every Friday afternoon
In spring and summer
There would be a sunset parade

All of Washington society came out
To see the show
The ladies in their light summer dresses and straw hats
The officers in their brilliant uniforms
Diplomats and heads of state
Even then-vice-president Richard Nixon came

It was a grand sight
For the spectators
But for the men who had to march
In their woolen dress blues
Under the broiling sun
It was an ordeal

I would hear the awful plop
As some marine fainted
And his rifle casing spilled upon the grass
After the ceremony we would rush
Up the stairs into the barracks
And some of the men would vomit
Into the toilet bowls

MARINE BARRACKS, 1952

We would lie exhausted in our bunks
Sweating from every pore
While in the commandant's garden below
We could hear ice tinkling in a glass
Or a society matron's
High-pitched laugh

Our pain gave pleasure
To a privileged few
I learned then
What every revolutionary has learned since
The world is a divided place
It's divvied up
Between the haves
And the have-nots
We were being trained for war

APRIL 19, 2016

Eleanor C.

Eleanor C. was drunk
As usual
She had locked herself
In her bedroom on the second floor
She wouldn't talk to anyone
Not even if you banged upon the door

When the first guests arrived
For a cocktail party
David, her husband
Was standing on the roof
He was trying to get in through a window
To the bedroom he shared with her

Oh, hi, he said
As if it were the most natural
Thing in the world
For him to be
Standing on the roof

Eleanor has a terrible cold
She can't come down, he said
As more guests started to arrive
Your could hear bottles rolling on the floor above
How sad, one of the guests replied

Suddenly there was
A great swooshing sound
Eleanor appeared
At the head of the stairs
Her hair was all disheveled
Her skirt askew
Why Eleanor how lovely you look
The same guest said

This was the world
In which I grew up
Nothing seemed to make any sense
At the same party
Ralph D. and I
Stood on the front porch
To admire the starry night sky
I thought we were sharing
Some awesome experience
When he fell
Flat on his face
In the grass
On the front lawn

Now Ann
Eleanor C.'s daughter
My brother's ex-wife
Calls me from time to time
From the rest home
In California where she lives

It's quite exclusive, she says
In her snooty manner
There are only five other patients here
Nothing ever changes
For some people it seems
I haven't heard from her
For more than fifty years
She wants to reminisce

Luckily, she has dementia
So she can't remember anything

Michelangelo

David! David!
Moaned Eleanor C.
As she writhed upon the couch
I knew her husband's name was David
So I asked if that was whom she meant
Her eyes popped open
She fixed her gaze on me
Not my David
You fool, she snapped
Michelangelo
She closed her eyes again
And leaned back on the couch
David! David!
She resumed

They went to see
Who's Afraid of Virginia Woolf?
And walked out
After the first act
Nobody we know
Behaves that way
They both agreed

APRIL 22, 2016

Love

We kissed in the apple orchard
Beside his house
At night
In the rain
What ecstasy
It almost makes up for the pain
That came afterward
Why can't love stay
Why are we all doomed
To oblivion
Is he dead whose lips I kissed
I'm sure he is
The only thing that's left
Is memory
And soon that will be gone too

APRIL 25, 2016

66 Pinckney Street

Catharine H. was a great lady
A true Boston Brahmin
The first one
I had ever met
She introduced me to
A world of grace and charm
Such as I had always wanted to enter
But only read about
In books by Henry James

She was whimsical
When she spoke
There was laughter in her voice
Once I was sitting on the chaise
In the front parlour
Of her house at 66 Pinckney Street

She was opposite me
At her writing desk by the window
Busily scribbling ink-stained notes
From a leaky fountain pen
I idly picked up an ivory letter opener
That was lying on a table nearby
On it was carved a polar bear
Oh, look, I said, a polar bear
Catharine H. looked out the window onto the street
Where, she asked
Then laughed at her own foolishness

The last time I saw her
Was in a nursing home in Brookline
She was a wraith of her former self
All beauty gone
She couldn't speak
Her musical speech had turned into guttural groans
When she saw me
Her eyes brightened for an instant
With their accustomed merriment

I did a portrait of her
Sitting on the same chaise
I had sat upon
She was wearing a golden dress
With Japanese blossoms painted on it
All the while, Moonbeam, her cat
Watched warily
The plaster was chipped
The walls could have used
A fresh coat of paint
No matter
She was regal
Imperious
It's one of the best paintings
I have ever done

I gave the painting
To Ruth W. and Frank L.
On the occasion of their marriage
Recently, I asked
If I might have a photograph of it
Frank L. refused
Without knowing what I was doing
I had consigned a lovely lady
To the care of a cruel jailer
I've got her under lock and key, he boasts
According to him, she's in storage
God knows where
I hate to think
Of the tortures to which he has subjected her
Far worse than those she faced in life
The ravages of old age
For all I know he might have murdered her

He's been known
To commit such crimes before

MAY 1, 2016

Molly H.

Molly H. fancied herself a liberal
She was a wild Irish woman
With a tongue like a knife
Her husband, Mark H.
Was the head of Harvard Law School
Women's Suffrage
Sacco and Vanzetti
Opposition to the war in Vietnam
Civil Rights
I'm sure she led the charge
If she were alive today
I imagine she'd probably trumpet
Homosexual rights

She didn't feel that way in the Fifties
Are you a homosexual, she asked me
With pronounced distaste
She was the Chairman of the Board
Of the Poets' Theatre
I was a writer in residence
I didn't know how to reply
I'm trying to deal with it, I meekly said

Molly H. thought nothing
Of using my words
As a weapon to injure me
It's almost funny
If it weren't so sad
How quickly some people's opinions change

Things may be different now
For some of us
The pain
Remains

APRIL 21, 2016

The Living Theatre

Julian Beck and Judith Malina
Were pacifists
They believed it in their core
Once Judith was beaten up
By two policemen at a peace rally
He didn't lift a finger to help
That was the moment when Judith realized
How much she loved him

APRIL 19, 2016

The Paper Bag Players

What was it about the Paper Bags
I enjoyed so much
They were metaphorical
The Princess was
Bad King Sorehead's daughter
He wore a jumble of boxes upon his head
She wore a plain cardboard box instead
On the lid of it was a painted smile
When the flap was up
She was happy
When the flap was down
She was sad
It turned into a frown
All in an instant, just like that
It was great theatre
But real life too

Remy Charlip was a postman
Delivering mail
He wore a shiny black cap
As I remember it
His letters were tissue paper
As bright as a butterfly's wings
He wondered if indeed
He was a postman at all
Or just a butterfly
Delivering mail

APRIL 11, 2016

Shirley Kaplan

I didn't know you were
In the Marine Corps
Shirley Kaplan said
She is one of the people
Who started The Paper Bag Players
Did you enlist, she asked
I said I had
Why, for God's sake?, Shirley Kaplan said
I wanted to get killed, I replied
It didn't happen
Thank God for that, she said
I've got to run
Love you
Goodbye

APRIL 19, 2016

Life

Henry M. was surprised
I had written I wanted to die
It's true
From a very early age
I wanted to leave this world behind
I'm an old man now, I still feel the same way
As with all feelings
I also feel the opposite
Life was a terrible thing
To waste on me
I've tried to make the best of it

APRIL 23, 2016

Freddie Herko

I

I'm still in love with Freddie Herko
Dead fifty years or more
I took a photograph of him
At that first moment when our glances met
I took hundreds of photographs of him after that

I look at them
And fifty years ago was yesterday
I'll meet Freddie tomorrow
And we'll take more photographs
And more and more
I could never get enough
Of the sight of him

Freddie! Freddie!
I cry out
He doesn't hear me now
He didn't hear me then
Fifty years is a long time
To live with only memory
I can't possess him now
I couldn't possess him then

How sad to see
Such beauty spilled upon the ground
I heard someone is writing a book about him
What could he know
He never held him in his arms
On New Year's Eve
When Freddie had to go to another party
He never took his photograph

MAY 1, 2016

II

Freddie Herko was once
The fairest of men
One of Andy Warhol's
Ten Most Beautiful Boys
When I saw him last
It was impossible to recognize
The beauty that he once was
His looks were lost to drugs
His cheeks were sunken
Many of his teeth were missing
It was in this state that he offered himself to me
I declined
He later committed suicide

In the eyes of some
That made him a saint
The fiftieth anniversary of his death
Was celebrated last year
At the site of his martyrdom
I did not choose to attend
The wreck of a human being
Made him a legend

I wrote these lines
As I lay in the sun
On Drew N.'s deck
Once again, as always
I had to crawl upon the boards
In order to get up
I'm an old man
I've stayed the course

I am not a legend
I am not famous
No celebrations will be held for me when I die
I'm just the wreck
Of another
Human being
With unwanted
Memories

MAY 11, 2016

James Waring

The winter of 1977
Was a sad time for me
I had to sell my house in Nantucket that year
To pay off debts
I left the island free and clear
I left the island penniless

I moved to New York
Friends gave me a place to stay
During this time
I did whatever work I could get

James Waring died
In the fall of 1976
I loved Jimmie
And more than that
I respected him

They had a memorial service
At Judson Church
David Vaughan and Al Carmines
Sang *I'm Following You*
Wherever you go
Whatever you do
I want you to know
I'm following you

The words haunted me
They haunt me still
In that desperate winter of 1977
I would stand
In the snow and slush
Waiting for a bus
To take me somewhere
I didn't have a cent in my pocket
I didn't know how I would survive

I'd hear the words of that song
Inside my head
Wherever you go
Whatever you do
I want you to know
I'm following you

I felt as though
Jimmie had sung them just for me
He kept me alive

MAY 28, 2016

Robert Indiana

Robert Indiana is my friend
We never speak
Even though
We live on the same island

I met him more than 50 years ago
He was Robert Clark then
Looking for a name
Like Tennessee Williams

After that
We bumped into each other
From time to time
We would exchange a few words
Maybe have a meal together
With Paul C. and Manfred I.

He came for afternoon tea last summer
It was as if we had been close
All of our lives

He's dying now
I am too
He did the sets for
Red Eye of Love
When we did the straight play in North Haven
I liked them so much
We reproduced them for the musical

Now it looks as though
The show will have a longer life
Than either of us
We're joined at the hips
For eternity
Whether we knew
Each other or not

MAY 1, 2016

Edward Gorey

People are surprised
When I tell them
I knew Edward Gorey
I guess I knew him
As well as anyone
You couldn't really know at all
We did seven shows together
Actually we were quite close

Most people think of him
As some sort of spectral wraith
Or a ghastly apparition
That's not the way
I saw him at all
I thought he was silly
In a most delightful way
That was his charm
Like a loveable, eccentric uncle
Or someone's favorite maiden aunt

APRIL 19, 2016

High

I'm high on something
Could it be life
I've never felt this way before
Like Coleridge on opium
When he wrote
Xanadu
And dozed off
Before he reached his pleasure dome
Or Emily Dickinson
When she wrote
Her dear little poems
In her Amherst mansion
I'm not sure she was so lovable
She seems to me to have had a spine of steel
Do you suppose
There was something
In those recipes

I've never shot up
I've never sniffed the white stuff
I've always wondered
What it feels like to be stoned
Now I know
I've become an addict
Of immortality

APRIL 19, 2016

Solitary Confinement

What is it about me
That makes it impossible
To communicate
Hear me
See me
Look at this
I'm always shouting
But I never get any response
Or not the response I want

We seem to be
Sealed off in our own
Little worlds
Little spheres
Bumping against each other
In the dark

Phil C. doesn't know me at all
Mr. Goodhue is a lost cause
Although he's been kinder to me lately
He's a sort of genius
You can admire that
His brain's so crowded
He doesn't have time
For anyone or anything
When I tried to bring my death to him
By struggling to take a walk
To the new house he's building
He wanted to talk
About his neighbor's dogs
Invading his chicken coop
And killing his hens

I'm alone all the time
I've no one to talk to
Except myself
And the whole world
And Jude

It's impossible
To get inside another person's mind and soul
We're all sentenced
To lives of solitary confinement
Within our own skins
As Tennessee Williams said

What's left
We can try
To let another person know
We care for them
That's about all
Jen D. and J.R. do that for me
Maybe Phil C.
I guess I'm lucky
I have three people
I can count on

Most people probably
Have none

APRIL 21, 2016

Possession

I've been possessed
That's what this book
Is all about
Like Salem's witches
Whose love of god
Turned into hate
Whose possessions
Became a means of possessing
Their neighbors' property
Men died for such calumny
Poor Giles Corey crushed with stones
His bones broken
What an awful fate

I hope no one
Ever dies for me
Possession has set me free
Poetry's the source
Of love
And liberty
Not remorse

APRIL 21, 2016

WILLA K., 2011

Willa K. (A MELODRAMA)

I've painted the background
Orange, she said
It's much cheerier that way
What could have possessed her
What thought obsessed her
Willa K. had been my friend
For fifty years or more
She asked me to paint her portrait
And I did
Lovingly, I thought
I should have known
What would happen
Willa K. always had to have
The upper hand
What a fool I was
How could I foresee
A painting would be the tool
She'd use to murder me

APRIL 19, 2016

Philippe Petit

Philippe Petit taught himself
To walk the tightrope
By walking on trees
As a child, he would walk
From one limb to another
Making a tour of the French Countryside

He showed us how
He had walked
Between the two towers
Of the World Trade Center
Before it was destroyed by terrorists

He drew a line upon the ground
Then he retraced his own footsteps
We followed, stumbling, after him

We walked
On earth
Where once
He had walked on air

MAY 1, 2016

Joe C.

Joe C. and I
Met as strangers
On a street corner
In New York
You had to speak loud
To be heard above the din

What are you doing now, he asked
He looked tired and worn
Nothing much, I answered him
I'm moving into a new apartment
It's a duplex, very grand
It has six rooms
Could I come and live with you, he asked
I was taken back by his request
I never thought he cared for me
Oh, no, that's impossible, I said
We tried it once
It didn't work out

I felt I should say something more
You do understand, I said
Sure, was his reply
Before I could say another word
He was gone

Two weeks later
I received a telephone call
To tell me Joe C. was dead
He had committed suicide
By jumping out of a fourth-story window
At the 64th Street McBurney YMCA

He did it on my birthday
Each year I cannot help
But remember

APRIL 23, 2016

Joe C.'s Song

I woke up this morning
To the sound of raindrops falling
I didn't know that you were leaving me
I didn't know
The raindrops told me so
And I called out your name
As I listened to the rain

That's all I can remember
Of Joe C.'s song
His song is unfinished
Inside my head
Just as his life was also unfinished

AUGUST 3, 2016

Paul S.

In later life
Paul S. came to live with me
I couldn't believe
My good luck
As a young man
He was one of the best-looking
People I had ever seen
I met him first
In a glass corridor
On 13th Street
He must have been
About eighteen years or so
I thought I would faint
At the sight of him
As usual we were not lovers
I never had sex with him
That seemed to be the rule
As a matter of fact
I was a little bit
Afraid of him
He died of AIDS
My one regret
Is that he did not let
Me take care of him
While he was suffering
He turned out to be
A kind and generous friend
Everything I have
I owe to him

FOR PAUL, 1994

I buried him
In the rain
In the orchard
By the house he had enabled me to buy
I spread his ashes on the ground
There were charred white chunks of bone in them
When I looked for him next morning
There was nothing there

MAY 1, 2016

Elzbieta C.

How could you
Do this to me
Elzbieta C. said
I'd painted her portrait
In a bright red dress
It hangs in André B.'s office now
Afterwards I heard
She'd sit and stare at it
For hours at a time

I've had bad luck with portraits
I seem to drive my subjects into fits
Frank L. took scissors
And cut his into little bits
And as I said before
Willa K. painted the background orange

I'm not alone in this
Didn't Madame X beg John Singer Sanger
To destroy the painting
He had done of her
Now it hangs in the Met
What irony

Elzbieta's dead now
For many years
All that remains
Is the painting I did of her
In my old age I try to paint
Only people whose looks I love
I feel it's safer that way
But that doesn't make any sense
I loved Frank L.
Willa K. and Elzbieta C.

ELZBIETA CHEZEVSKA, THE RED DRESS, 1993

Why did they all
Take my love for hate
Could it be
They couldn't see
How much I cared for them

I just assumed
It was myself
Who didn't know how to love

APRIL 22, 2016

Barney H.

Barney H. was my hero
He rescued me
When I was washed up
On an enchanted isle
We made masques
He was Prospero
I was Ariel

Barney H. is no hero of mine
He let me drown
When it suited him
He fired me
Although he did it in such subtle way
I didn't realize I'd been axed
Once again you'd think
He was Prospero
Setting Ariel free

How can a man
Be two things at once
We all are
We're good and bad
We're black and white
We're day and night

Good and bad
Black and white
Day and night
Depend on each other
For their existence

I believe it is what is known
As a conundrum

MAY 1, 2016

Transgender

Cindy B. is now Cidny B.
He really doesn't seem
Much different from her
Cindy B. and I wrote a musical together
Called *Islands*
Cindy always felt
She was a man
Trapped in a woman's body
I don't want anyone to feel trapped
If Cindy B. is happier as Cidny B.
That's fine with me
Except I get confused
I always call Cidny B., Cindy B.
He says that's all right
I must learn a new language

MAY 1, 2016

Two Davids

One David yelled at me
In his heavy Scottish brogue
The other David lectured me
His tone was more gentle
But he was equally severe
They live together
They are like fraternal twins
They both felt I needed correction
Out of an assumed friendship they were willing
To take on the onerous task

Maybe I am the monster
They make me out to be
Even monsters have feelings
I don't like to be yelled at
Or lectured to

If I'm the sort of person they say I am
They shouldn't want me for a friend

MAY 5, 2016

66

Russell Janzen

Russell Janzen might be a great dancer
I hope so
For his sake
As well as mine

As a very young man
Not more than thirteen or fourteen
He appeared in two events
On North Haven

In *The Tempest* he was
Some sort of wind or sprite
He danced trailing
Yards of white China silk
It wasn't much of a role
But he rehearsed
With great intensity
He also appeared
In one of our musicales
He sang a love song
Called *My Best Pal*
By Michael John LaChiusa
The song was written
For another man
But Russell sang it to a dog.

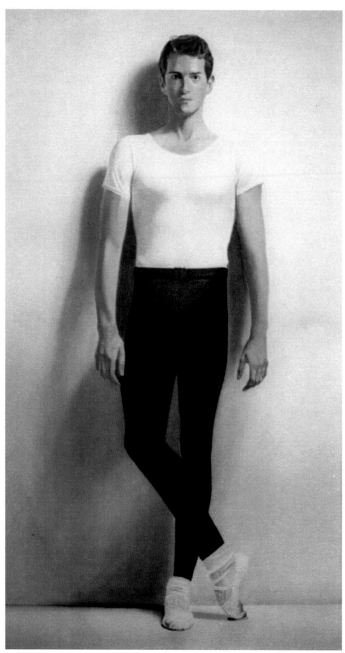

RUSSELL JANZEN, 2011

I've followed his career ever since
I've worried through
Times of injuries
I've read every review
I basked in his accolades
Each award he won
I felt I'd won too
I even did his portrait

Be great, I said
The last time I talked with him
I'm trying, he said
What more could anyone ask

APRIL 13, 2016

Can You Hear Me Out There

Can you hear me out there
I always ask
It frustrates me
To go to poetry readings and lectures
Where I cannot make out
One single word
Usually because
They are using microphones
Which have a voice of their own
That seems to be at war
With the human voice

It annoys me
We have all these means of communication
But nobody communicates
Look at our national political scene
It's a disgrace
We've given a platform
To people who
Have nothing to say

No matter their words say nothing
They are reported endlessly
We've made an industry
Of having nothing to say
If we could all just take
A vow of silence

For one minute
Maybe we'd hear something
I guess that's probably too much
To ask in this Tower of Babel
We call home

Nowadays it's the man
Who says nothing
Who has everything to say

APRIL 22, 2016

My Closest Friend

Jude lies on the lawn
And rolls upon his back
With his forepaws in the air
His teeth gleam
He seems to be smiling in the sunlight
But I can't be sure
He is my closest friend
Yet I do not know
What he thinks or feels
He is a mystery to me

APRIL 21, 2016

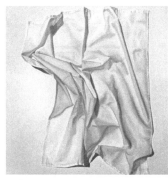  

VARIATIONS ON AFTER THE BATH BY RAPHAEL PEALE, II, V, III, 1996

Breath/Death

If poetry is synonymous
With breath
When the poetry stops
Will my breath stop too
I'm afraid of that
Not really afraid
If life stops
There will still be my book
My plays and poems
My photographs and paintings
To show for it
Maybe they'll take up my breath
When I leave off
How glorious
To become a poem
Instead of just
Another human being

APRIL 25, 2016

If You Write a Book

If you write a book
You'll quickly see
How little regard
People have for you
I'm too busy right now
I'll read it sometime
I promise you
And then you never hear from them again

You wonder why
You wrote the book at all
If it was to share
The secrets of your life
You needn't have bothered
Your secret's safe
With nearly everyone you know

APRIL 30, 2016

What's the Trouble

We seldom take time
To think
Or feel
It's a lovely afternoon
I'm going to take Jude
And go for a walk
Maybe we'll see a miracle or two
Along the way

They happen frequently
If only we would
Stop
Listen
Look
All of life is some sort of miracle
If you think about it
Take the shoes I'm putting on right now
To go for my walk
They're a miracle
Have you ever thought about shoes
I mean really thought

Lucy D. was the miracle today
I met her on the road
She sang me
A Scottish melody

MAY 1, 2016

A Short Walk

I took a short walk today
Just down to the roadway
And back again
With Jude beside me all the while
I'm tempted to try a longer distance
But I don't know
If I'm up to that
I want to get in shape
For some great event
Is it something wonderful
Or merely death
That old thing
I have already experienced
So many times before

APRIL 22, 2016

Kelli O'Hara

I got three songs by e-mail today
Two of them were mostly mine
Kelli O'Hara was singing them
What joy
What bliss
Maybe I could be a songwriter too

I'd like my songs to be
As simple as an Irving Berlin tune
All Alone
Just breaks my heart
What'll I Do
Makes me think
Of Fred Herko and Joe C.
Who both committed suicide
By jumping out of windows
I myself would never do
Anything as rash as that

It's too much fun to hear
Kelli O'Hara singing your songs

APRIL 23, 2016

A Whole Lifetime

A whole lifetime
In just a few weeks
That's how fast
I've learned to speak
A madman's rant
Lies on my tongue
I keep telling myself to stop
I simply can't
Don't lock me up
Put me away
I've got much more I want to say
I have to finish
This can't go on much longer
Fever! Fever! I might cry out
And beg for some surcease
I'm glad Jen D. doesn't hear me
My pain is my release

APRIL 22, 2016

Fire

Flames die out
They turn to ashes
And are extinguished

I'm no longer working at a fever pitch
One or two poems a day, that's all
I am at peace with poetry

I'm still afraid of fire
My grandmother
Was burned
In a gas explosion
She was scarred for life
She spent two years
In a hospital having skin grafts
Her face was spared
The rest of her body
Was twisted and gnarled
Like the bark on an old tree

In Nantucket
I stood in the parking lot
And watched Straight Wharf Theatre burn
On the day I took it over
I was conscious of other people watching me
As all my hopes and dreams
Went up in flames
I sold my house
I paid my debts
I moved away
I began again

Although, I too, like my grandmother
Had been scarred for life

A fire can be brought back to life
By blowing on it hard
That's what happened to me
Slowly I started to flame again
I burned for a little while

Eventually
The fire abated
I thought it would go out
Now it's roaring once again
How many times can I be
Consumed by flames
I'm only one man
There's just so much to burn

If, as Artaud said, the only art
Is signaling through the flames
I've burned enough
When will I turn to ashes
When will I be extinguished

It's something I fear
Yet pray for, nonetheless

APRIL 23, 2016

Death's Interesting

Death's interesting
I find the whole process fascinating
It's kind of fun
The doctor smiled
No one had ever said
Such a thing to him before

APRIL 22, 2016

Phew!

I'm glad that's over
I couldn't have stood much more
By the end
I was writing
A poem a minute
It was like flames
Licking up at me
I couldn't stomp them out
I went for the walk
That Jen D. suggested
Mr. Goodhue rescued me
By his indifference once again
He's like a world
Contained within himself
He doesn't take me seriously
There's some healing in that

One last word
Before I stop
I'll put it in a bottle
Throw it out to sea
If anyone should find this
I'd like them to know
I'm all right
Once again
I have survived

APRIL 25, 2016

Making Poems

I love writing sentences
With words in them
The girl ran down the hill
That's a sentence
What's more
It contains
Three perfect iambs

There's a rhythm to life
I'm only beginning to comprehend
Take all my words and sentences
Cut them up
One by one
Put them in a hat
Mix them up
Paste them together
Any way you choose
They'll still come out a poem
Try it
You'll see what I mean
I guarantee
My words are indestructible

How curious
I'm only writing down
Words I hear
Inside my head
Have I discovered a new haiku
Am I a mad inventor
Or some crazed scientist
I'm writing poetry
By indirection

Marcel Duchamp would have known
What I am talking about
He also made green boxes
From which you could pull out
Seemingly unrelated things
The act of pulling them out
Assembling them in some sort of order
Gave them meaning
They were art by indirection too
M. C. Richards would have understood
John Cage certainly
Also Merce Cunningham
They made art by chance
They used the *I Ching* as their guide

Words are sounds
That should be dropped into a poem
The same way you'd drop stones into a pond
They have their own weight and heft
I've held them in my hand
I've measured them
They send out ripples

Some people might say
What I do
Isn't poetry at all
Just prose
Prose with affectation
A slur against the Noble Estate of Literature

I disagree
I may have no reputation as a poet
Or anything else for that matter
I'm not a member of any inner circle
I'm not going to stop
Writing sentence
With words in them
Until I'm blue in the face
Or dead

MAY 1, 2016

Ronin

Have you ever heard
Of a ronin
I never heard the word
Before yesterday
Apparently a ronin is some sort of samurai
Who did not commit suicide upon his master's demise
Instead he wandered through the world
Writing poems about his own death
Which he would sell to keep himself alive
I guess I'm a ronin too
Fancy that

MAY 1, 2016

My Feet Are Sore

My feet are sore
I found a cure
Johnson's Foot Soap
Soaks away foot misery

The directions said
To put warm water into a bowl
Sprinkle the powder over it
Then soak your feet
For fifteen minutes

I did this
I didn't have a bowl
So I used the bath tub
I sat on the rim of it

I also didn't have a clock so I counted instead
One
Two
Three
Four
Five
Up to sixty

Try doing this fifteen times
Often my mind would stray
And I'd lose count
What was the name of the medicine
Johnson's Foot Soap
Yes, that's it
Remember
Maybe you can use it later

I'd resume counting
Four
five
Six
Sometimes I'd rub between my toes

Once again I'd lose count
Damn!
I'd have to start all over again
One
Two
Three
Four

Afterwards I undressed
I weighed myself
I put on fresh clothes
I fed Jude
I put clean water into his bowl
I squeezed orange juice
I took my pills
The routine never changes
Breath in
Breathe out
You're doing fine
Tick
Tock
Tick
Tock

So life goes by
One second at a time
One
Two
Three
Four
Drip
Drop
Drip
Drop
Until finally
Time has a stop

Everything's in meter
Just like a poem
I must have known that before
But never understood
I know now
At last
That's why I have become
Much to my surprise
A poet

APRIL 25, 2016

Inebriate of Air

Inebriate of air am I
Jeanette S. reminded me of the line
How great, how true
I'm drunk
On the first bloom of spring
Intoxicated
With warm summer days
Green grass
Blue skies
Ocean black
Glistening in the sun
I almost faint
From autumn's fiery red
And tipsy fall
Into winter's bed of white

Death's the price
We have to pay
For so much wonder
How sad to depart
And leave all earthly things behind
I'm ready for the journey
Into the blackness from which I came

Like Emily Dickinson
I've tasted air
So sweet upon the tongue
What a light weapon
To wield against so dark a foe
One breath's enough
To live
Through an eternity
Of death

APRIL 20, 2016

Profligate of Talents

If one thing didn't work out
I'd try another
I didn't spread myself too thin
I mastered every art I tried
There was so much time to fill
And I filled it with work
At 88 I am making more
More and better
Than I ever made before
The cost I've had to pay
Is being alone
Day after day
Year after year

Of course, occasionally
I have to stop and feed myself
Nowadays, someone has to give me
A ride to the grocery store
To purchase supplies
I'm grateful for their effort
They make on my behalf

Do all artists
End up like this
Alone
Still making poems and paintings
I think they do
Was it worth it
Weighing everything
I would say
Yes

MAY 1, 2016

The Telephone I

The telephone rang
I answered
An official voice came on the line to say
The IRS has filed suit against me
For further information call
609 something
I didn't get the rest
Phil's away
I turned to Jude for counsel
Jude, we're probably going to jail, I said
Jude was mute
As is his want
He didn't answer
If he could speak
I think he'd say
That's all right
Haven't we lived in solitary confinement
For several years now

MAY 1, 2016

The Telephone II FOR KAREN WEBSTER

A man called today
You called this number, he said
Maybe I had
I asked who he was
Actually, it's my relative's number, he said
I asked their name
You must know their name
He answered angrily
You called this number
I said I call a lot of numbers
I couldn't remember all of them
I'm going to report you to the FBI, he said
Please do, I replied
I'm grateful for any attention I can get.

MAY 5, 2016

The Telephone III

I thought of making
A telephone call to say
I've nothing on my mind
Do you
No. Well then
Goodbye
The conversation is ended

The telephone
Is my enemy
I make a call
A voice comes on the line to say
I've dialed a wrong number
Would I look up the number
And dial again
I look up the number
It's exactly as I thought
I redial the number
The call goes through
Or, what is even worse
I dial a number
I wait for along time
Nothing happens
Again
I have to redial again
Again, the call goes through
Such mechanical failure
Drives me insane

Oh, I forgot to say
I call John M. at least
Fifteen times a day
He never answers
Talk about mad

I just called Kevin McD.
On the first call
A whirring sound
Came on the line
On the second call
I got the same whirring sound
On the third call
Nothing happened
On the fourth try
The call went through
I've got to laugh

Do you suppose
Alexander Graham Bell
Invented the telephone
Just to torment me

APRIL 20, 2016

Philanthropy

Most people want to make money
From their poetry
Me, I think that's a bad idea
The poems came free
They should be free
To anyone who wants to see or hear

People want money
For their poems or paintings
The result is
For the most part
They don't get published or seen

I'm a philanthropist with words
And paintings too, for the most part
I give them all away
The only problem is
I've now got the IRS to pay
I'd like to make a dime or two
Cancel all my debts
I simply don't know how
I've been poor all my life
Yet rich somehow
There's no changing now

I'm old and feeble
Hardly any worth
Except for writing poetry
And making paintings
We all know
Where that gets up

APRIL 22, 2016

Children's Voices

I heard children's voices
In the roadway
I looked out of my door to see
Who they were
Jude was just sitting there
He wasn't following them

I took my cane
And went out to see
If I recognized who they were
I saw them standing
At the bottom of the hill
Bright red caps, green scarves
Hello, I called
They didn't answer me

With difficulty
I made my way
Down the hill
I heard the squawking of chickens
In Mr. Goodhue's yard
Oh no, I thought
I knew that his neighbor's black dog
Had eaten several of his hens

I made it
To the bottom of the hill
I couldn't hear a sound
Where have they gone, I wondered
Suddenly they appeared again
Further on down the road
Beyond Mr. Goodhue's property
I now could see there was a black dog with them
Also a grown man

I couldn't walk any further
I started back up the hill
I saw Mr. Goodhue coming down
What are you doing here?, he said
I heard voices and I was afraid
They were disturbing your chickens
It's my neighbors, Mr. Goodhue said
Did they have a black dog with them
I said they had

It's my neighbors, Mr. Goodhue said again
Their dog killed my hens
What were they doing in my yard anyhow
I don't want them around

I was tired from my walk
I put out my arm for support
You're going your way
I'm going mine, Mr. Goodhue said
And left me to make it up the hill
On my own

You see what I mean
About indifference
As usual I got home all right
Mr. Goodhue knew I would
I told you he was maddening

I'm a tougher old bird
Than Mr. Goodhue's hens

MAY 1, 2016

The Prodigal Son

I always wanted
To put brush to canvas
Make a great swoop
A splash
I never did
I was too cautious
Painting, for me
Was a way of passing time
Each stroke a second
More strokes a minute
Then on to hours
Days and years
A whole lifetime of painting
Because I was afraid of life

Quite honestly, I never thought
I was any good
Or not good enough
David H. would have agreed
He loved my paintings
Then he hated them
Just as he loved, then hated me
He died of copying photographs, he snarled
I never understood

Now I look at my paintings
And wonder who painted them
They're strangers to me
They surprise me
By having a life of their own
No matter what
My own personal limitations

What a hard trick
To have gained life from indifference
They have survived in spite of me
What a price to pay
The hand that made them
Was the hand that turned them away

The prodigal son's come home
He's here to stay
I don't think he will ever
Go away again
Even though I know
That I myself
Their cruel father
Has got to go

APRIL 21, 2016

Philomena

Philomena knew
What it was
To have one's tongue cut out
I once saw a photograph
Of a production of *Titus Andronicus*
Kabuki style
When the actress playing Philomena spoke
Blood red ribbons
Came out of her mouth

I too have had my tongue cut out
It's grown back
By some miracle
I can speak again

MAY 2, 2016

Silence

George Brush was a Bible salesman
In Thornton Wilder's *Heaven's My Destination*
When he lost his faith
He lost his voice
An archbishop in Chicago died
He willed to George
A set of silver spoons
The heads of the Apostles were carved on them
When George received this bequest
He began to cry
He started to speak again

Guy Crouchback was a victim of World War II
In Evelyn Waugh's *Men at Arms*
He lay silent in an Egyptian hospital ward
Wrapped in bandages
Suffering from skin burns
Julia Stitch came along
With her silly chatter
And a jar of calf's foot jelly
Guy Crouchback also cried
He began to speak again

Joe C. was a real person
He was overwhelmed
By the sadness of life
He didn't speak for a long time
One day he was in a magazine shop or a grocery store
He overheard the proprietor's wife

Talking to a customer
How are the children, asked the customer
I don't know, the proprietor's wife replied
They've grown up now
They've moved away
We don't hear from them anymore
Joe C. began to cry
He started to speak again

Mimi B. was also real
Her father abandoned her in a hotel room
She was just a teenage girl
Mimi B. was overwhelmed with fear
She lost her voice
She wanted to become a cloistered nun
Then she met Russell B. and fell in love
She began to speak again

Life teaches us
All the reasons to be silent
Death teaches us
All the reasons we must speak.

MAY 26, 2016

WINTER HARBOR, 1969

Winter Harbor

I think it's one of my best paintings, I said
You've got to be pulling my leg, Phil C. replied
It's true
It's what I hope to achieve in art
Everything has been stripped away
Just sky
And sea
And an arc of snow
Nothing else
That's all you need to see
The painting was molded in a crucible
Over a fire of high intensity
I wish everything I make
Could be so simple

It's extremely difficult to be simple
You must expose yourself naked to the flames
Reality burns
Into intellect

APRIL 21, 2016

APPLE, 1985

A Secret

I cannot draw
That's my secret
In order to make a painting
I have to project
An image on the canvas

That's not wholly true
Actually, I can draw quite well
Some of my best paintings
Have been done out in the fields
I draw the shapes in pencil
Then I paint in watercolor over that
I once spent a rainy Sunday afternoon
Painting five apples in this same way

I wonder if
Eventually
Some scholar or archivist
Will try to compare my painting
With the images from which they were made
I'm sure there would be
Very little resemblance
Between the two

Why do I always say
I can't
When actually
I often can

MAY 11, 2016

A Final Altercation

This afternoon when I took a walk
Down to Drew N.'s workshop
I stopped on my way back
At the entrance to Mr. Goodhue's property
I wonder if he's at home, I thought
Then I saw his blue truck
I started to walk to Mr. Goodhue's house
Jude veered off
To the area where Mr. Goodhue keeps his hens
No, Jude, I said
Don't go there
You mustn' t bother Mr. Goodhue's hens
Jude obeyed me, something he seldom does
Then I saw
Mr. Goodhue's hens were standing by his front door
When they saw Jude
They ran away and hid

Mr. Goodhue came flying out of his house
His arms upraised
Go away, he shouted
I've told you I don't want you here
I turned to leave
I didn't want to depart in anger
I turned to Mr. Goodhue once again
I only came because
I had an idea of colors you could paint your floors
He'd asked me for ideas the night before

I'll get a rope, he said
I'll tie him to a rope
But there wasn't any rope handy

You should put him on a leash, he yelled
How could I put Jude on a leash
I couldn't control his pull
There was nothing more to say
I turned away
And sadly walked home with Jude

I don't know what to do
Mr. Goodhue and I
Have been neighbors for thirty years
He gets more eccentric all the time
He's bright and smart
As I have said many times before
But he always makes me feel
There's something wrong with me.

Is any relationship
Worth this much abuse
I doubt it
I tried to be his friend
I obviously failed
I'm resolved
I'll never set foot
Inside Mr. Goodhue's house again

It's a painful solution, I know
Especially
Since I have so few friends left
You have to avoid people who hurt you
Deliberately
When you are old

APRIL 30, 2016

King Lear

Lear learned
The world didn't care for him
It seemed evil and malevolent
That was just his point of view
The world didn't care
What he thought
It was indifferent
It had been here before him
It would be here after him
When he learned this lesson
Truly learned
It in his soul
He earned
Serenity

Will such serenity
Ever come to me
I don't think so
I am too filled with rage
At the world's indifference
But Lear
Was also filled with rage
Perhaps there is still
Some small chance
To learn
To earn

I don't ask for much
Serenity is such a simple thing
Why do we have to pay for it
With our lives

MAY 1, 2016

BOOK TWO

Dedicated to Micah Conkling

Eternity

When I die
There will be
No time for me
Time without time
Is what time will be
There is no time
In eternity

JULY 5, 2016

Roseanne B.

You'll probably have
The whole book done by suppatime
Said my cleaning lady, Roseanne B.
Your thoughts come so fast
You just have to get
Out of the way of them

Just think
One whole book
By six p.m.
I wish it were possible
To get a publisher so fast

JULY 5, 2016

Forgiveness

I thought I'd write
One book of poems
Then call it quits
I'm only beginning to realize
That's not possible
There is so much to write about

I go back thousands and thousands of years
My father
My mother
My grandparents
I had only one set of them
My father's father
Married my mother's mother
Unlike other people
My past is finite
My grandparents end
In a single couple
But behind that single couple
Extend countless other lives
My past may be finite
It's also infinite

I know very little
About my forebears
Some of it was heard
In hushed whispers
Behind closed doors
I know my father's mother committed suicide
I know he was raised by his sister
But that's about all I know

As for my mother
I probably know even less
Her mother ran a delicatessen
In Hell's Kitchen
She was in a gas explosion
Which scarred her for life
While she was in a hospital
My own mother feared she would be put
Into an orphanage
She taught herself
Not to reveal
Any emotions
Her education was hard on me
Everything connects
Everything interweaves
We never know
What will be the consequences
Of what we say and do

I sat on Main Street today
Waiting for a ride
As cars drove past
I thought of how many lives they contain within them
People loving people
People hating people
People hurting people
For vast eons of time

What forgiveness after all
There is not anyone who is not maimed by life
Forgive, forgive
It's all that we can do
In a world that has
No forgiveness for us.

Giggles

The sea is calm tonight
Did Matthew Arnold write that
It is the end of a lovely summer afternoon
I can hear children
Giggling on the lawn
As the long shadows of night descend
Life may laugh at us
But we laugh too
It's nice to end the day
With giggles

JULY 5. 2016

Poets and Misers

Poets with words
Are like misers with gold
They fondle each nugget
They bite into them
To see if they are the real thing

Poets with words
Are not like misers with gold
Misers hoard their treasures
In burlap sacks upon the cellar's floor
Or underneath their beds
Poets, on the other hand
Are spend-thrifts with words
They scatter them to the winds

If I had to choose
Between a miser and a poet
I'd choose the poet every time
Maybe that is why
Even though I am very poor
I am very rich

JULY 6, 2016

Writing Words

Writing
Words
One
By
One
Is
Fascinating
The
Whole
History
Of
The
English
Language
Is
Contained
In
Them
For example
Why does i with an s
Connote the present
Why does a w and an a with the same s
Connote the past
From
What
Gutteral
Sounds
Did
Speech
Evolve
And
How
Did
Those
Sounds

Assume
Meaning
So
That
Man
Can
Communicate
With
His
Fellow
Man
We
Know
Another
Person
By
The
Way
He
Sounds
We
Know
If
He's
Happy
Or
If
He's
Sad
But
Why
Over
The
Course
Of
Time

Did
Sounds
Take
On
Meaning

It
Is
The
Poet's
Job
To
Make
Us
See
Words
New again
I know that new
When grasped
Is known
I can figure out
That what's known is knew
But where do the Ks come from
Where do the ns
It's
A
Mystery
I
Might
Spend
A
Whole
Lifetime
Studying

I
Would

Like
Words
In
The
Sentences
I
Write
To
Take
On
A
Life
Of
Their
Own
I
Have
Used
Very
Few
Punctuation
Marks
But
I
Think
The
Meaning
Is
Always
Clear
Look
At
Each
Word
As
If

It
Were
Newly
Made

The
World
Becomes
New
Again
Whoever knew
It had so many wonders
Once knew is known
Everything
Is
Transformed
It's like spring
Overcoming
Winter's Death

JULY 6, 2016

Madness

If I am truly mad
What use is it
To write down words
The average man has no use for madness
He's satisfied
With things exactly as they are

Madness is a new continent
We've made voyages before
We've made vast treks across land and space
Why should we not probe
To the blackness
That is at the center of all things

Madmen are explorers
They tell and show us regions
We have never seen before
I'd like to be an adventurer
Into those unknown realms

Who knows what I might see
What constellations
What realms of gold
Van Gogh saw Irises
If I had to choose my life's occupation
I would choose a madman's lot

JULY 7, 2016

Suicide

I've been reading David Foster Wallace's
Infinite Jest
I called up a friend to find out
If he knew anything about him
My friend looked him up on-line and told me
David Foster Wallace committed suicide
He hung himself
He was forty-seven
That made me think
About my own futile attempt at suicide

At college in my senior year
I was confined to the infirmary
I had collapsed in a snow bank
A professor, Warner B., found me
And had me committed

For two days I lay unconscious
As they pumped fluid into me
I didn't say a word
I just lay there
Silent
The amazing thing was that
As I was stretched out on my hospital bed
I also seemed to be watching myself

There had been a disconnect
Between my mind and body
If my mind told my body
To raise my arm
Nothing happened
Instead of one being
I was two

While I was in this disoriented state
After lights out a young intern
Slipped into my room
Almost noiselessly
What's wrong?, he said, I'm here to help
There's nothing wrong, I said, what makes you think that
I can tell by the rate of your breathing, he replied

No, no, there's nothing wrong, I insisted
I couldn't see his face
He frightened me
After he had left the room
My mother called, hysterical
If you would only tell me what's wrong, she wailed
Perhaps I could be of some help

After my mother's telephone call
I went into the bathroom
I looked at myself in the mirror
For a long, long time
I took a razor blade
And tried to slit my wrists
I was a failure at that
Just as I thought
I was a failure at anything human

After I was released from the infirmary
My parents took me to Mexico
For three weeks to regain my health
We saw three bullfights
I thought of Ernest Hemingway
Everywhere we went
Mexico City
Vista Hermosa
Acapulco
Dolores del Rio appeared
She seemed to be
Mexico's patron saint

After I had graduated from college
I applied to the Navy's officer training program
I was refused
I had given the name of Warner B.
The professor who had committed me
As a reference
When he filled out the regulation form
He wrote that I was mentally unfit
To lead men into action
At first I was hurt by what he had written
But then I saw
He was only being honest

I enlisted in the Marine Corps
I wanted to prove my manhood
I wanted to show I could take almost anything
Either that, or get killed
The joke was on me
I wound up Honor Man in my platoon

JULY 9, 2016

Bob U.

Bob U. sent me a check
For seven hundred dollars
There was a note attached
He said he wanted to thank me
For all the things I had done for him
Throughout his life

Oh, no, I thought
Why would he have done such a thing
He must be dying
I called him this morning
I can't accept this money, I said

Please do, he begged
You've done so much for me
I just wanted to send
A token of appreciation
Before I die
I thought it would be easier
Than putting you in my will

Are you dying, Bob?, I asked
I am, he said
I can't get out of bed anymore
Is there someone there with you
Oh yes, I have two nurses

One comes to me from Monday to Thursday
The other comes from Friday through the weekend
Do they stay with you?, I asked
They stay until I fall asleep at night, he answered me

I didn't know what to say
Oh, Bob, I love you, was the best that I could do
John, I love you too, he said
Goodbye
Goodbye

JULY 9. 2016

Melville and Hawthorne

The greatest lovers among American writers
Were Herman Melville and Nathaniel Hawthorne
I'm speaking about lovers
People who talked soul to soul
Not Walt Whitman
Not love of boys
Not Zelda and F. Scott Fitzgerald
Not blighted romance
Certainly not Ernest Hemingway
Not attitude

Melville wrote *Moby Dick*
As a gift to Hawthorne
Hawthorne received the gift
And understood it
Something no one else did at the time

When Melville met Hawthorne
In Liverpool so many years later
They had nothing to talk about
By then, Melville was a grinding failure
Hawthorne had grown complacent
It was as if they had never truly known each other

But they did
They were lovers in the truest sense
I don't mean in any physical way
Although Hawthorne was beautiful
They loved each other's minds and hearts

It's sad
That such passion should end
In cold estrangement
On Liverpool's sweaty streets

Walt Whitman

You have to hand it to Walt Whitman
He was a fraud
On a grand scale
For three years during the Civil War
The good grey poet made a tour of Washington's hospital wards
Tending the sick and dying
He wrote letters home for them
He brought flowers
Jars of jam and honey
A pie he'd baked
A few coins
He also stooped
To kiss and fondle them
It must have been awful
To be brushed by his long beard
Back then his actions were considered good deeds
He bore on his shoulders a nation's grief
Now we would have locked him up
As a dirty old man

What sort of language did people speak
In America
In the 1860s
What did people think
When they read *Leaves of Grass*
When Walt wrote about Man's Love of Man
He was writing about Man's Love of Man
They made Walt Whitman out
To be some sort of saint
Good for ol' Walt, I say
He had his cake and ate it too
All saints have feet of clay

JULY 10, 2016

Tying My Shoes

It takes me
Such a long time
To tie my shoes
I sit on the edge of my bed
I put one leg over the other
When I can reach my shoes
I have to find the laces, then I have to tie them
Loop over loop
The whole process is exhausting
When I am finished
I lie back upon my bed
To catch my breath

Nothing should be easy
But does it have to be this hard
Just to get through the day
They should give some sort of medal
To those who survive

JULY 13, 2016

Charlotte G.

Charlotte G. is the lady
Who mows my grass
I watch across the field
As she makes her rounds
On her blue tractor

Charlotte G. is not well at all
She has cancer, I believe
She is all skin and bones
And yet, there she is
Wearing a straw hat
Tending to my fields
In the broiling sun
I think it is wonderful
To behold
Such devotion to nature
Most men harshly trash their space
Charlotte G. tenderly cares for it

I can hardly believe
It is Charlotte G. mowing my fields
I hear she is feeling much better lately
Maybe there is the possibility
She'll recover her health
She's mowed my fields
For more than thirty years
Death can have no victory over her
Each year
When the earth returns to green
She'll have her triumph
Over the blackness
That encompasses us

JULY 13, 2016

Dana B.

It wasn't Charlotte G. I saw
It was Dana B.
I walked down to the meadow
To say hello to Charlotte G.
I fell down in the grass
Dana B. had to help me up
It was a struggle
But I made it after all
Charlotte G. and I
Are both dying at the same time
She no longer mows for her regular customers
She only mows her own fields
She says it's made her feel better
Dana B. has now taken over my fields
Life goes on
Whether or not
We are a part of it

After I had written my two poems
I read them to Dana B.
He was gruff and in need of a shave
You don't know me, he said
I don't know you
I love you anyhow

JULY 13, 2016

Deeds of Love

I must stop writing poems
Death's the only end for me
At this rate I could go on and on
Endlessly
Maybe I should just call it quits
While I am still ahead
Or alive
As the case may be

There's only one story to tell
Anyhow
Eden found
Eden lost
First we feel
And then we fall
First we fall
And then we feel
We not only tell
But live
Over and over again
We never seem to get the point
But strive in offices of love
How we may lighten each others' burden
In our mutual share of woe
Writers such as Joyce
Poets such as Milton
Have told us
Over and over again

It's such a simple lesson
Why do we refuse to learn

JULY 14, 2016

The Ferryman

Take your time, the ferryman said
He wasn't Virgil helping Dante into his bark
So he could make a tour
Of the underworld
Although I looked the part
I have white hair
I'm unsteady on my feet
I am a poet too

The ferry was only going
To Rockland, Maine
There will be time
And there will be time
I answered the ferryman
He looked confused
He must have thought
I had taken leave of my senses
T. S. Eliot would have known
Exactly what I meant
There will be time
And then there will be time
You can look it up
In *The Love Song of J. Alfred Prufrock*

How many poets and poems
Can one ferry-boat contain
As it makes its run
From Vinalhaven
To Rockland, Maine

JULY 15. 2016

A Love of Poems

During the spring of our senior year
Tom O'C. and I
Drove from Hanover, New Hampshire
To Barre, Vermont
To see a touring production of
Oklahoma! With an exclamation point
We went in my old battered jeep
The top was down
So we had to holler
The entire way

Who wrote
All are naked, none is safe
I shouted
Marrianne Moore, he shouted in return
It's my turn now, he went on shouting
Blear eyes faded from blue
That's easy, John Crowe Ransom, I exulted
Right the first time, he continued to shout
I didn't think you'd get that

We were dizzy
With poetry
We were both on fire
With the sound of words
I've never made
Another journey happier than that
Oh, to be young again
Oh, to have someone with whom to share
My love of poems
Shouted above
The traffic's din

No More/Evermore

No more
A sunset
Over the lake

No more
A sweet clear voice
Singing in the evening
Over the waters

No more
No more
Life cries out

Evermore
Evermore
Life answers itself

JULY 16, 2016

I Can't Put

I can't put
My head to pillow
A poem interrupts my rest
Joy and pain
Are both intertwined
I want the poems
I also want
Some sleep

JULY 16, 2016

BEDROOM, SEPTEMBER LIGHT, 1994

I Am Afraid

I am afraid
To set foot to stairs
One step is a poem
Another step is another poem
At this rate
I'll never get to bed

JULY 16, 2016

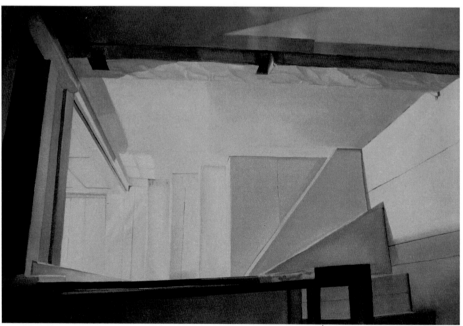

STAIRCASE, SEPTEMBER LIGHT, 1993

So Much Living

My brain is like an enormous warehouse
Boxes and boxes of useless information are stored there
Yellowing clippings from *The Standard Star*
An announcement of my parent's wedding
My birth announcement
Announcements of my graduation
From college and the Marine Corps
My brother's baby book
Soon all these boxes will be burned
They'll be thrown on an ash heap
As I will too
So much for life
It goes up in smoke
The smoke fades into the atmosphere
Whoever would have thought
That so much living
Could just disappear

JULY 18, 2016

The New York Times

Since death has given me
A new set of spectacles
It's easier to read
The New York Times

Its pages are filled with accounts of
War
Murder
Pillage
Rape
Political skullduggery
Police brutality

Here it all is
Right on the front page
There is an account
Of someone named Cain
Who slew his brother Abel
What odd names
In a sordid tenement flat
On the lower East side
There's a photograph of Cain
So he is marked for life

Take away the spectacles
If this is what I've got to see
I'd rather not see at all
Death might have fixed my sight
But I prefer the illness to the cure
How sad to lose one's sight
How sadder still to see

JULY 18, 2016

Four Composers

There are four composers
Living in my former home
Their works are going to be played
By the Cassatte Quartet
On Tuesday in the Union Church

I pounced on them
I wanted to have someone
With whom to talk
They're very young
They're very nice
They're very polite
But they didn't have
A word to say
Will I never meet anyone
With whom I can have
A dialogue

JULY 18, 2016

Shakespeare

Shakespeare fell in love
With a younger man
He wrote his sonnets for him
He said he would make the youth immortal
He said that in his lines
The youth's beauty would never fade
All of which came true
The only thing is we are not sure
Who the youth was
Or what he thought

He probably said
Gee, Pops, that's great
I mean, thanks a lot
I'm really touched
But I'm a young man
And, let's face it, you're getting on in years
Can't we just be friends
I'm sure that Shakespeare was willing
To settle for that

Of course, all the prudes and pedants
Made out that the boy
Was not a boy at all
He was a lily-fair maiden
Or a dark-skinned one
We've got to face the facts
Shakespeare loved a young man
The young man probably did not return his love
It's an old story, often told
But never told so well
Before or since

One of the ways
Shakespeare made himself immortal
Was by making himself
Ridiculous
Tell me life is not a joke
I too have fallen in love with a younger man
I didn't want it to happen
But it did
What will become of us

JULY 19. 2016

Sonnets

I want to set myself a harder task
I want to write sonnets, as Shakespeare did
I've got to learn the form
Fourteen lines
With a rhyming couplet at the end
I'm sure I'm up to that

I've got all the raw materials
I know my youth's more fair
Than Shakespeare's ever was
Or Beatrice for Dante
If you prefer a woman to a man
If Shakespeare and Dante could make poetry out of their loves
Think what I can do with mine.

JULY 19, 2016

A First Attempt

Here's the first sonnet
Don't laugh at me
When I look into his eyes I see
Blue skies
Ocean
Infinity
I've done it wrong already
I'm still writing in my old form
I'll have to start
All over again

JULY 19, 2016

A Second Attempt

I've gotten Shakespeare's sonnets out
Maybe they will give me a clue
Here's a good one
That age thou mayest in me behold
When yellow leaves, or none, or few
Do hang upon these boughs
Which beat against the cold
Bare ruined choirs where late the sweet birds sang
No, that won't do
I can't copy Shakespeare
But I've got the iambic pentameter honed
If my words were as good as my meter we'd be home

I can't get by with Shakespeare's verse
I've got to strike out on my own, for good or worse

JULY 19, 2016

A Third Attempt

He came to visit me on his bicycle
He was wearing slim jeans, an olive tee-shirt
I can't remember if I said you're beautiful
I know I must have thought it—that's four lines
I'm only beginning to get the knack
I've got six more lines ahead
Writing sonnets is like a long-distance race
How can an old man like me keep up the pace
That's nine, three more laps to go
I'm winded, but I'm doing great
Now I'm missing just one more rhyme
I'm determined to cross the finish line

I don't need H_2O, I need a couplet
That would taste better than any droplet

JULY 19, 2016

Immortality

I know that love has been writ many times
By poets far more clever than I shall ever be
What chance have I against their skill
I'll probably make a botch of poetry
Just as I have made a botch of everything else
My art is meager, but my heart is full
I may not know how to draw the bow
But why not aim for the silvery moon
Shakespeare, as usual, hit the mark
Why should that deter others with less ability
If Shakespeare bestowed immortality on his young man
Damn it! That's what I want for mine

To learn my art, I don't have long
Right or wrong I must sing my song

JULY 19, 2016

SONNET TWO

His Reward

I'd like to think his reward for knowing me
Would be the same sort of immortality
That Shakespeare conferred on his young man
I'm ridiculous, I know, I have to laugh
The desire is very real, the skill is not
It's nice to have ambition, even though
Your dreams might far exceed reality
Columbus would never have found a new land
If he'd been fretful and stayed at home
You've got to sail the seas of chance
You've got to scale the mountain's highest peak
To seek the sort of love of which I speak

It's the same old story, wouldn't you know it
My love's the very best, I am the worst to show it

JULY 19. 2016

SONNET THREE

I'd Like to Sing

I'd like to sing my love, don't ask me to
You wouldn't like what you heard at all
I fear I'd make a dreadful squall
My pitch is not perfect, it's always off
I have no sense of rhythm, and besides
I am truly tone deaf in both my ears
What a dilemma in which to find myself
I want to sing of love but can only croak
Lessons would not help me the least little bit
I tried to play upon the violin
To no avail, I made an awful screech
I'll have to settle for plain old speech

How sad to want to sing love's old sweet song
When the most right you can do is wrong

JULY 19, 2016

154

SONNET FOUR

Frank O'Hara and Vincent Warren

Frank O'Hara loved Vincent Warren
He wrote a slim book called *Love Poems* for him
It's a collector's item now
Later Frank was killed in a tragic car accident
On Fire Island—at the time he wrote his poems
He was forty-six, Vincent was twenty-two
When Frank presented the poems to him
Vincent did not know what to say
He was a young dancer with his own career to think about
He moved to Montreal where he became a premier danseur
With the National Ballet of Canada
By the time Frank died they had grown apart

Did Frank and Vincent fail at love, that depends
Because what Frank wrote was true, their love never ends

AUGUST 19, 2016

Perfection

It's all so perfect because he's so perfect
I love his looks, his voice, his hair
The silver earrings that he wears
In each one of his ears
Can love be perfect? No, it can't
But if not perfect there's always hope
That man can get outside his own being
And care for another as he cares for himself
When we do that we make a start
At being human, isn't that the goal
We never can make one out of two
A futile attempt's the best we can do

Perfection lies within the lover's eyes
Most men see earth, the lover sees the skies

JULY 19, 2016

SONNET SIX

A Fleeting Glance

In matters of the heart you cannot trust a poet
Poets will swear to almost anything
Did Shakespeare really love a fair young man
Or was it someone he passed upon the street
Their eyes met just for an instant, a fleeting glance
And then they went their own separate ways
Never perchance to meet again
In crowded bars or pick-up joints
Their love often isn't love at all
But just a spark of their feverish brains
It doesn't take much to set a poet's mind on fire
They have been known to weave yards of whole cloth
Upon the looms of their desire

For most, love is a game one seldom wins
For poets, love's loss is when the game begins

JULY 19, 2016

I'd Like to Find

I'd like to find some bright young man
Upon whom I could bestow my hopes and dreams
What I have done has not been done for me
All these years or wearisome work and toil
Have yielded me almost nothing at all
After I am dead, my work might have some worth
There is no way of ever telling that
But more than gold, there is the gold of memory
After I have been many years deceased
Eaten by worms, moldering in my grave
If there is someone who thinks fondly of me
That would be more than I have ever asked

Wouldn't you know it, so close to death
Is the moment I inhale my first deep breath

JULY 19, 2016

SONNET EIGHT

I Met Him Only Yesterday

I met him only yesterday
I started the sonnets today
I've already written seven of them
They come so fast because
I like to think my love's so deep
I don't want to do anything to spoil it
Most loves end, I'm sure of that
The lovers quarrel or they meet someone else
I want my love to endure
I have so little time
Certainly his love can last
A few days, that's not much to ask

He's young, I'm old, we've made a start
Let's not let life tear us apart

JULY 19, 2016

SONNET NINE

A Formidable Foe

Eight sonnets is not much to show
For all the effort I've put into them
Most are probably not very fine
At least not fine enough for a fine young man
I can't imagine the perfect gift for him
Besides, Shakespeare bought out all the shops
He swept the shelves clean of merchandise
What chance have I to compete with him
If I say my love is more fair than his
No one will believe me anyhow
What is my word against the Bard
For him it was easy, for me it's hard

Shakespeare, Shakespeare, what a formidable foe
Dull time has burnished him with a golden glow

JULY 19, 2016

Blue Skies

My love is more fair than a day in June
His teeth are more white than the whitest pearl
When I look into his eyes I see blue skies
Whoever wants to write guff like that
I love my love because he is alive
He lives, he breathes, that is enough for me
Why pour on the hyperbole
What's real is better than a poet's raving
He's fine, he's true as tempered steel
One look at him and anyone would feel
All the possibilities of life come true
In him lost Eden is created anew

My love is not a fiction conceived by me
He has his own hard firm reality

JULY 19, 2016

Improper Form I

I do not want to shield him
From all earthly harm and woe
I've never known how
To shield myself
How could I shield him
I want him to feel
The lash of spring rain
The burn of summer's sun upon his face
I want him to feel
The nip of autumn's frost
The chilling bite of winter's snow
I want him to feel everything

Spring, summer, winter, fall
My love, my love, must have it all

Improper Form II

The last sonnet I wrote
Was not proper form at all
I said what I wanted to say
I got it right outside the form
If form's the enemy of truth
Then form has got to go
All I want is hard reality
I can hold within my hand
A rock, a few pebbles
To remind me of the earth

Hard earth beneath my feet, that is the reason why
I am able to touch the sky

JULY 20, 2016

Music

A Concert on Vinalhaven

The musicians intertwined
With their instruments
Man and music made one
Their bodies were not still
Their heads jerked
Their mouths were agape
Their legs twitched
You could feel the music
Moving through them
To hear music inside one's head
And then make others hear
That is the soul of art

The world
The heavens above
All made indivisible
The music of the spheres
Played for us
By musicians intertwined
With their instruments
In Vinalhaven, Maine

JULY 20, 2016

I Never Told My Love

I never told my love
I kept it inside myself
Where nothing grows
I thought if I told the truth
There would be hell to pay
The hell was not telling my love
By keeping it inside of me
It died of neglect
From not watering

July 20, 2016

I Had Tea

I had tea
With a good-looking
Young man
That about
Sums it up
I wrote these
Last few poems
As a sort of exercise
I was having fun
With poetry
The poems are all
False but true
I might wish
That they were true
But alas, they're false
False as false can be
The simple truth is
I never heard
From the young man again
We didn't even share
A second cup of tea
I would say pity me
But the demand exceeds the need
I'm not worth anyone's pity
You are supposed to laugh
Or cry, as the case may be

JULY 21, 2016

A Bargain

I read my love my poems
The world didn't end
We both survived
Let's be good friends
Our whole life through, I said to him
Yours will be long
Mine is nearly done
However few days I have left
I'd like to spend them
Knowing you

July 21, 2016

Just Think

Just think
I have a friend at last
I could almost cry
For joy
There are no secrets
That he doesn't know
We're friends
For ever more
I'm sure of that
We shook hands on it
I don't need
Any other bond

JULY 21, 2016

Farewell, Marco

Farewell, Marco
I've found someone
More fair than you
I still remember
The debt I owe
You gave me my life
I'll always be grateful
To you for that
But life goes on
I'm sorry
I've called you five times
You never answer

Farewell unrequited love
Hello, unrequited love
It's the only love for me, it seems
Old men must live
Within their means
Old men must love
Within their dreams

JULY 21, 2016

André B.

André B. is a gentle man
He gently turns the pages when he reads
I think he was hurt by his life
As I have been hurt by mine
Maybe that is what has bound us together
Over such a long stretch of time
Our parents
Our siblings
Even life itself
Have tried to destroy us
We have survived

We have survived
In spite of
Heartbreak
Unbearable loss
We go on making things
We remain creative
We put up boards
To ward off
The hurricane

We make sure
Our torches work
In the event
We are plunged
Into eternal blackness
No sign of light
A terrible stillness
Everywhere

Light! Light!
It's going fast
Soon night will darken the entire world
That is why
I write these lines
In the fading dusk
I want to leave a testament
To friendship
Something lasts
Something endures

JULY 22, 2016

Phil C.

In the midst of
A hot and busy summer
Phil C. takes time
To type my poems
Why does he do it
He does not seem to be
Especially interested in the poems themselves
When I tell him
They might make money
He just smiles
How can I repay him
I've left him all
That I have left to leave
Again, he just smiles
He doesn't seem to think
There's any value in that either

Now he is helping me
Organize a reading of my poems
I just don't get it
Could the thing that I have missed
Be love
That's the only explanation
I can think of
But why for me
He doesn't even seem
To like me very much
Everything is a mystery

I've never known
How to repay love
I thought it had to be
Coin for coin
That doesn't seem to be
The case in this situation
Could it be that
Nothing for nothing
Is
All for all
Why not let the worry go
And accept the love instead

JULY 22, 2016

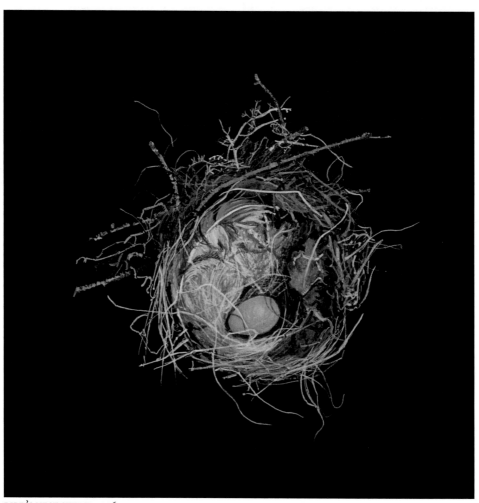

BIRD'S NEST STUDY, 1996

A Hummingbird FOR ANN SACHS

I found a hummingbird
Dead
On my kitchen floor
I don't know what
To do with him
I guess I'll pick him up
In a paper towel
And consign him to
The compost heap

He's beautiful
A long black beak
Blue feathers
Black wings

I think of other
Bright and glittering things
I know
Eventually
They all will be compost too
They'll rot to earth
To feed
The garden

Don't be sad
The hummingbird
Still flutters and flies
With his black wings and blue body
He sucks the morning glory
With his long black beak
Because I wrote this poem.

JULY 24. 2016

Poetry is a Sound

Poetry is a sound
You hear inside your head
You can hear it while
You are doing the dishes
Or cleaning the sink
I hear it now
Almost all the time

JULY 25, 2016

Blackness

Jude is so black
I can't see him at night
Jude! Jude! I call into the darkness
As usual
He never answers
It's only when I sit
On the door sill
He comes to me out of nowhere

JULY 23, 2016

THE LISTENER IN THE SNOW, 2012

Wayne C.

Wayne C. was the best looking boy
In our high school class
One summer, my family
Rented a cottage
On Lake Morey, Vermont
I wrote Wayne C. and asked him
To come and visit us
I didn't think there was
Any chance he'd come
When he wrote back
To my amazement
He told us the date of his arrival

Wayne C. for ten whole days
I couldn't believe my luck
Each day, all day
We'd swim in the lake
But then, Wayne C. thought up a game
He would dive from the landing dock
I would dive from the float
About thirty feet away
We'd meet in the middle
Underwater
We'd put our arms around each other
And we would kiss
For a long, long time
It was not like
Any game I'd ever played before
But whatever Wayne C.
Wanted to do
I was up for that

When Wayne C. and I
Returned to high school that fall
He acted as if
We had never met before
Imagine
My new best friend
Treated me as if I were
A stranger

Wayne C. was planning
A camping trip with Harold S.
Can I come too, I asked
Why not, Wayne C. replied
When I never heard anymore
About the camping trip
I asked Wayne C. what was happening
He said you really don't want to come
It's not your style

That afternoon
When I walked home from school
I cried the entire way
I remember I saw
A break in the clouds
I thought of God
I was very religious then
Later that evening when I told my father
What had happened
He said what a fine son I was
I seldom got any praise from him

Migsy W. also loved Wayne C.
I met Migsy W. first
When we were both children
We used to play together
To while away the time
At Rotary baseball games
You're too fat
Those were the words
Wayne C. used
To put Migsy W. down
She began to diet
She became anorexic
Years later when she married another man
She could hardly make it down the aisle
She was so thin
The weight of her wedding dress
Upon her shoulders
Was unbearable

Jump ahead in time
Although Migsy W. had three children
She divorced her husband
She had become an alcoholic by then
Her family put her in
A rest home near Poughkeepsie
One evening, late at night
Migsy W. escaped
When the police found her
Several hours later
On Poughkeepsie's dark streets
She didn't even know her name

The police put Migsy W.
Into the local hospital
The hospital, in turn
Called her parents
There was no time
For her parents to get to her
Just tell her we love her
Was all her mother could say

I've thought a lot
About Wayne C.
I don't know what
Has become of him
I don't know where he lives
Or if he even lives at all
I don't know whether he is
Alive or dead

He was the killer
In our high school class

JULY 27, 2016

Damned World I

I've taken
Just about all
I am going to take
From this
Damned world

I hurl
My weapons
Against the foe
Words
Sentences
They fall
Off him
Like pistol shots
Fired by Lilliputians
Against Gulliver
They leave no more trace
Than a little sting

I am having
An anxiety attack
I fear
The end
Is near
I do not want
To give up the fight
Life
Or
Death
Who will have
The final word

It's not much of a question
To dwell upon
I already know
The answer

JULY 29, 2016

Damned World II
The Sequel

It's summer
I made
A root beer float
With vanilla ice cream
To comfort me

JULY 29, 2016

My Father's Birthday

Tomorrow
July 30th
Is my father's birthday

What was he like
I wish I knew
I think he was a kind man
I think he was also sad

We never
Really knew
Each other
I think
That's one reason
He was sad

If a son
Cannot know
His father
Can anyone
Know anyone

JULY 29, 2016

Victory

I'm finding it
Harder and harder
To communicate
I have so many details
Inside my brain
I can't get them out
I pronounce each word distinctly
I think I'm heard
But then the person
I am talking to
Asks me a question
I realize they haven't understood
One word I've said
I have to start
All over again

I've been reading
David Foster Wallace's
Infinite Jest
I think he had the same problem
I am talking about
Also Van Gogh
Details, details
One detail leads to another
And then there is another detail after that
They swim like fishes
Inside my head
It's madness
I said to Tim C.
Do you realize

This is the madness
That I have been
Talking to you about
He said he knew
He said he understood
Maybe that is why
I have always loved Tim C.

Antonin Artaud
Started the whole thing off
He was talking about
The sort of madness
That makes a man
A true artist
That's what I've always wanted
Now I find
Madness is not madness at all
My brain is clear as a bell
Why was I frightened
I can't tell where it all will end
Maybe in an insane asylum
Like Artaud and Van Gogh
Maybe in victory
Who do I know
Who has ever won
A victory over life
I hope, I hope
It will be me

JULY 26, 2016

Acknowledgements

I acknowledge with deep gratitude friends and neighbors who helped make this book possible. Special thanks to Barbara Kinder, Hugh and Sue Martin, Phil Crossman, Jeanne Bineau, Gay and Alvin Gamage and John Morton.

I am also very grateful for the support of Ann Ash, William Beadleston, André Bishop, Alison Hildreth, the Gordon and Janzen Families, Roger Morgan and Ann Sachs, Charles and Caroline Pardoe, Diane Proctor, Ilene and Don Vultaggio and Monica and Ali Wambold.

I would also like to thank Paige Parker and Bridget Leavitt for book design and production and Philip Conkling for editorial advice.